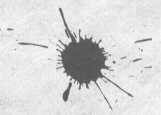

Scholastic Children's Books,
Euston House, 24 Eversholt Street,
London, NW1 1DB, UK

A division of Scholastic Ltd
London ~ New York ~ Toronto ~ Sydney ~ Auckland
Mexico City ~ New Delhi ~ Hong Kong

Some of the material in this book has previously been published in *Horrible Histories The Rotten Romans* and *Horrible Histories The Ruthless Romans* first published by Scholastic Ltd, 1994

HARDBACK EDITION ISBN 978 1407 19561 2
SCHOLASTIC CLUBS AND FAIRS EDITION ISBN 978 1 407 19853 8

Printed in the UK by Bell and Bain Ltd, Glasgow

2 4 6 8 10 9 7 5 3 1

www.scholastic.co.uk
horriblehistories.movie

HORRIBLE HISTORIES
THE
MOVIE
ROTTEN ROMANS

HORRIBLE HANDBOOK

■SCHOLASTIC

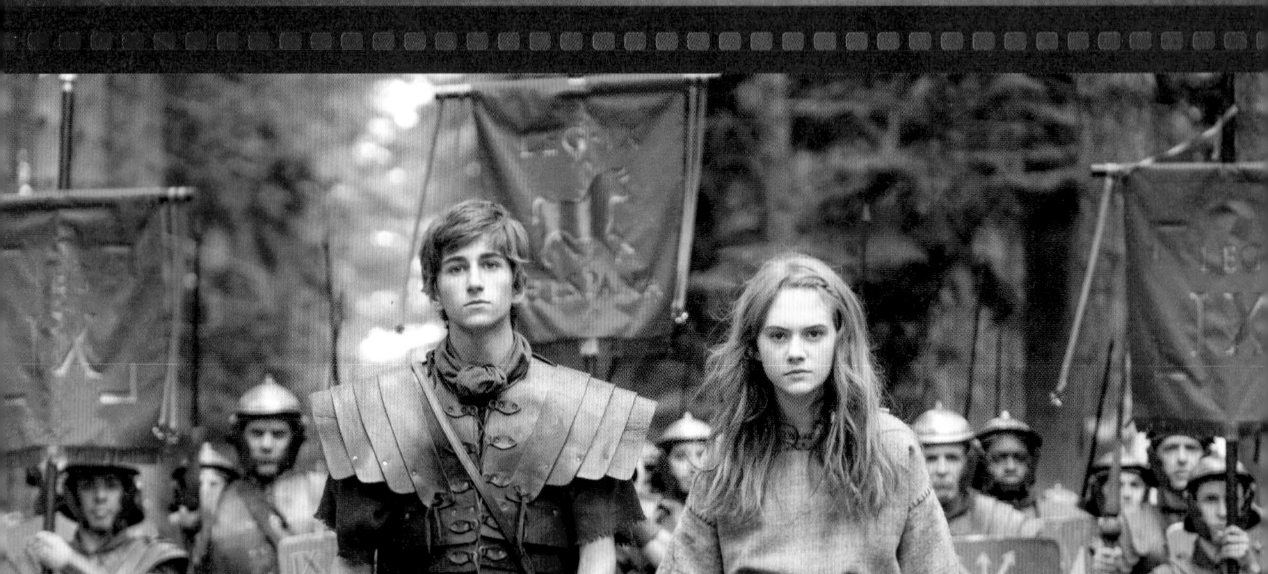

CONTENTS

INTRODUCTION

Roman teenager Atti is forced to join the Roman army when one of his clever schemes falls foul of Emperor Nero. He is sent to miserable, cold, wet Britain (that weird stain on the map) where the natives are revolting – quite literally.

Things go from bad to worse when Atti is captured by Orla, a feisty teenage Celt desperate to prove herself as a warrior. Atti uses his Roman know-how to help Orla save her gran who's been kidnapped by a rival tribe and then, thanks to Orla, narrowly avoids a very sticky end in a bog.

Meanwhile, a furious Nero is determined to crush the rebellion, led by Boudicca, Queen of the Iceni. Atti re-joins his Roman troops and discovers they are preparing for an historic showdown with the Celts at the Battle of Watling Street. Atti's brains could save the day but they could also spell disaster for Orla as the two new friends find themselves lined up on opposite sides of the battlefield.

SOME PARTS OF THIS STORY MAY NOT BE 100% ACCU-RAT!

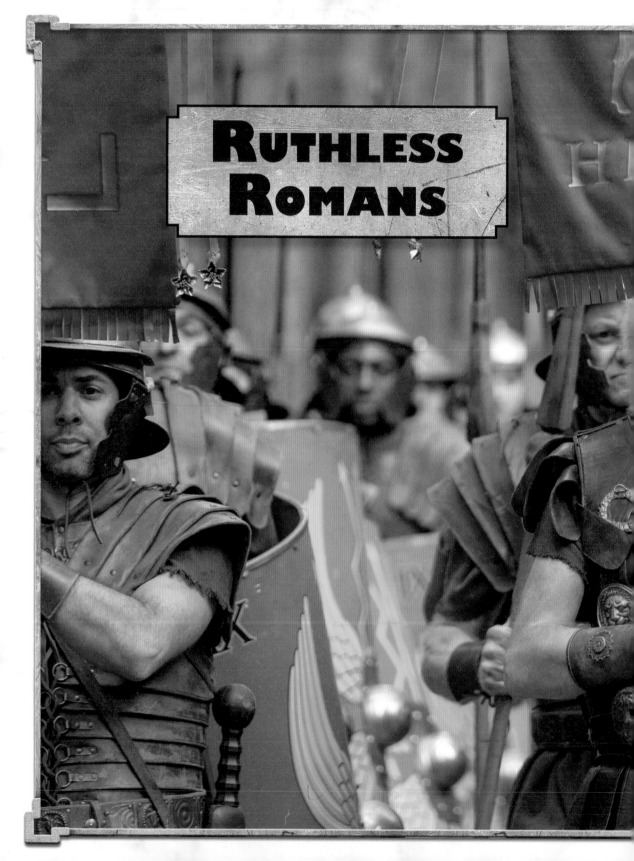

RUTHLESS ROMANS

RUTHLESS ROMANS

Teachers and history books try to tell you how great the Roman Empire was… They often use the word "civilised" to describe the Romans – that's the opposite to "wild".

Yet the Romans killed people for fun! The Romans made murder into a sport. They built wonderful buildings like the Colosseum, filled them with happy Romans and then massacred thousands of people and animals for entertainment.

They did lots of other ruthless and disgusting things too. They created "emperors" with an "empire" which smashed everyone in sight … and many who were out of sight too. It all started back in the distant mists of time in Italy…

Terrible Timeline

EMPEROR VOM VOM

753 BC
Early Roman farmers live in a place called Latium. This is where the city of Rome was built.

509 BC
The Romans are fed up with their cruel king, Tarquin. They throw him out and rule themselves (that's called a Republic).

264 BC
First of the Punic Wars against Carthage in North Africa. Result: Rome 1 Carthage 0.

218 BC
Hannibal of Carthage attacks Rome with elephants. He can't capture Rome but he rampages around Italy terrorising people.

202 BC
Scipio takes charge of the Roman Army and beats Hannibal. Result: Rome 2 Carthage 0.

146 BC
Carthage is wiped out completely.

55 BC
Julius Caesar invades Britain for the first time for the country's tin, copper and lead.

44 BC
Julius Caesar is elected dictator for life – then murdered!

AD 43
Claudius gives orders for the invasion of Britain ... again!

AD 60
One tribe in Britain, the Iceni, rebel. Queen Boudicca leads them in battle against the Romans and kills thousands of them. Then she is defeated and she poisons herself.

AD 80
Julius Agricola completes the invasion of Britain (except for the Picts in Scotland).

14

BOUDICCACA

AD 122
Hadrian starts building a wall across northern England to keep out the Picts.

AD 235–285
Fifty-year period with over twenty Roman emperors, mainly because they keep getting murdered.

AD 401
Roman troops are withdrawn from Britain to defend Rome from attack.

AD 410
The last Romans leave Britain.

AD 1453
End of the Roman Empire.

PLOPICUS

ATTI

(played by Sebastian Croft)

Most Roman boys enjoy mindless violence, but Atti prefers to spend his time with his nose stuck in a scroll. Atti's life changes forever when one of his clever schemes causes a stink with Emperor Nero. Suddenly, he finds himself shipped off to Britain to join the Roman army. When Celt teenager, Orla, captures him, he must learn to use his Roman "know-how" to survive.

"We need to be clever, we need a plan."

ROMAN "KNOW-HOW"

The rotten Romans ran the world for a long time. There are still signs of their life around today. You probably use things the Romans invented every day, without even knowing it.

Concrete

Books
(like this one!)

Battlefield surgery

Catapults
(wait, they might have stolen that one from the Greeks)

HORSE WEE

Orla shows off her speedy sword skills.

As well as useful inventions, there are some rotten things in Britain today that we can blame the Romans for. They brought them here. Things like...

PLOPICUS

Stinging nettles

Next time you sit on one, you can cry out in agony, "Oooh! The rotten Romans!"

Cabbages and peas

The sort of vegetables your parents make you eat because "they're good for you." Next time you hear that, you can say, "The Ancient Britons lived for a few thousand years without them, so I can too!"

Cats

Yes, blame the Romans for that mangy moggy that yowls all night on the corner of your street and keeps you awake. When teacher tells you off for yawning in class, say, "Don't blame me – blame the rotten Romans!"

I HATE CATS. THEY THINK THEY'RE SO PURR-FECT!

ATTI'S PARENTS

Antonius and Julia (played by Tony Gardner and Katherine Jakeways)

Atti's parents want their son to get stuck into Roman life with all the gore and glory. When Atti is forced to join the Roman army, Atti's dad is happy that he has finally found himself "a proper Roman job". Once they visit Atti in rainy Britain, they eventually realise that's there's nothing wrong with being a bit brainy.

"A proper job for a proper Roman!
Well done lad."

EMPEROR CLAUDIUS
(played by Derek Jacobi)

Emperor Claudius arranged to have a little island invaded. It is Britain. Despite this successful campaign, Claudius still gets it down the throat. His wife, Agrippina, feeds him poisoned mushrooms. Afraid Claudius will recover she sends a doctor to tickle the back of the Emperor's throat with a feather. The feather has been dipped in a deadly poison. That finishes him off.

EMPEROR VOM VOM

Claudius became ill with diarrhoea ... well, it's not surprising really. Agrippina had fed him poisoned mushrooms!

"I am done for. P-p-p-poisoned."

EMPEROR NERO
(played by Craig Roberts)

After the murder, ahem, death of his uncle, Emperor Claudius, Nero is crowned the new Ruler of the whole Roman Empire (even that stainy bit). The rotten Roman emperor everyone loves to hate, he has a horrible habit of murdering people. From gruesome gladiators, to cruel crucifixions, the only thing he loves more than a Roman bath is a bloodbath!

"Oh goodie, some mindless violence!"

NASTY NERO

There is no doubt that Emperor Nero was mad. For a start, he told people he was a god and anyone who refused to call him a god ended up in the sewers. During his rule, Nasty Nero did some really rotten things…

I'M A CHRISTIAN, GET ME OUT OF HERE!
Nero had Christians persecuted cruelly…

- They would be tied to a post, covered in tar and set alight.
- They would be covered in animal skins and thrown to hungry, wild dogs.
- They were crucified in large numbers.

TERRIBLE TUNES

Nero loved singing and performing – but no one was allowed to leave the theatre, even though Nero went on for hours and hours. It was rumoured that some men were so bored they pretended to be dead so they could be carried out of the theatre.

Foul Fact
Nero dressed in the skins of wild animals and attacked human victims – unbearable!

AGRIPPINA
(played by Kim Cattrall)

They say there are two sides to every coin, and what's better than one with your face on it? Thinking she can rule the empire through her weak and wicked son, Agrippina poisons her husband, Claudius, and Nero becomes emperor. Little does she know that nasty Nero has a different idea of how to deal with mummy dearest.

"You will not believe what just happened to me."

Nasty Nero plots to have his mother murdered.

SYCOPHANTUS
(played by Alex Macqueen)

Sycophantus is Emperor Nero's assistant and biggest fan. Well, not really, but he does fan him with a big fan. That counts, right? Sycophantus loyally serves Nero to death – literally.

"Brilliant! Quite brilliant!"

FOUL FEASTS

The rotten Romans loved their food, and would often have large feasts and banquets where lots of truly foul food was served. Here are some food facts to make your mouth water or maybe turn your stomach… Peacock tongue anyone?

During such feasts the guests could eat so much that they had to be sick! Guests would empty their stomachs and then keep right on eating!

The Romans had some sickly sauces. One was made from rotting fish guts, which the Romans would add to their meals a bit like you use tomato ketchup today.

HORRIBLE HISTORIES
THE MOVIE
ROTTEN ROMANS

PARTY LIKE IT'S 60 AD

THERE'S NO PLACE LIKE ROME

Welcome to Rome, with its beautiful blue skies, betrayal, conspiracy and death!

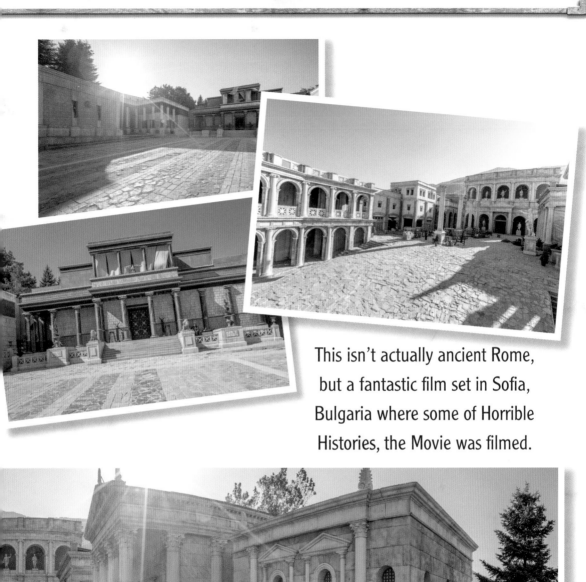

This isn't actually ancient Rome, but a fantastic film set in Sofia, Bulgaria where some of Horrible Histories, the Movie was filmed.

CATUS DECIANUS
(played by Alexander Armstrong)

Catus is the procurator of Roman Britain and that means he can do whatever he wants. Boudicca's husband, Prasutagus, left half his kingdom to the Romans, but Nero decides he wants the lot. Catus sends his Roman troops in to loot the Iceni tribe. This annoys Boudicca so much that she decides to start a rebellion. When the Roman cities start to burn, Catus quickly runs away to Gaul.

"You really should have read the small print."

Catus had the gall to take Boudicca's stuff.
He then ran away to Gaul!

GORY GLADIATORS

The rotten Romans loved a good fight. Thousands of people would come to arenas to watch gladiators fighting. Sometimes they battled each other, and sometimes they were up against wild animals.

Gladiators were men (and sometimes women) who fought in front of an audience – a bit like some footballers today. But footballers aren't given swords and spears and nets to fight with. Though it's a nice idea…

Most gladiator fights stopped when one fighter was too wounded or exhausted to go on. But some of the fights went on till one of the gladiators was dead.

If a fighter gave up, exhausted, he could surrender. The emperor would then decide if he deserved to live or not. The crowd would usually tell him by screaming, "Mitte! Let him go!" or "Lugula! Kill him!" The emperor would signal his decision with his thumb. Thumb down for death – thumb up for life. And we still use that sign today.

GLADIATOR SWEAT

OH GOODIE, SOME MINDLESS VIOLENCE

To the Death

Proper gladiators cost a lot of money to feed and train. Posh Romans paid the bills and put on gladiator shows for the poor Romans. In return, the poor Romans voted for them. No one would spend all that money to see it wasted with a few short, sharp chops. In fact, the top gladiators fought like today's boxers – the crowds loved watching their skill and betting on who would win. Those top gladiators lived to fight again.

Foul Fact
The Romans used to sell gladiator sweat as a beauty treatment, they would sell it in souvenir pots.

ALWAYS GOOD TO SPLASH OUT!

HORRIBLE HISTORIES
THE MOVIE
ROTTEN ROMANS

GLADIATOR IN TRAINING

CRIME AND PUNISHMENT

Right, punishments! The Romans didn't mess about when they caught criminals. Punishments were painful. Very painful. And many of them were made into shows for the public to watch. So really, Atti got off easily after he gave Nero horse wee. Other Romans weren't so lucky…

Stealing crops – throttled for thieving a few field things. (Try saying that fast with a mouth full of stolen cornflakes.)

Setting fire to your neighbour's house – you'd be burned alive – after being whipped. This is a good example of Romans "making the punishment fit the crime".

Calling someone a nasty name (slander) – you would be clubbed to death. Of course, you could escape the clubbing if the name you called someone was true!

Rotten Roman Army

The Romans were fearsome warriors and they were famous for their well-organised and deadly army. But the Romans were the best army in the ancient world because they used something their enemies didn't. The Romans used their brains!

The Romans won a lot of fights because they had good stabbing swords and armour and ... zzzz! Excuse us while we fall asleep. Never mind the armour and the weapons. What you really want to know is that they were ruthless. They were nasty, cruel and vicious. That's why they won!

Those warriors who weren't killed in battle were captured and ensalved by the Roman army. The conquered peoples around the

empire joined the Roman army and conquered other peoples who joined the Roman army and conquered ... and so on until they ran out of conkers.

DECIMUS MAXIMUS

(played by Lee Mack)

Centurion Decimus is on his last mission before he retires and wants to get it over and done with as quickly as possible so he can return to beautiful sun-kissed Rome, with its dry Mediterranean climate and never-ending summer … ahem! Luckily for him Britain is an easy posting, nothing ever happens. Or so he thought…

"Ah, sweet Rome!"

GAIUS SUETONIUS PAULINUS

(played by Rupert Graves)

Paulinus is a mighty (and muscly) Roman General who loves nothing more than battling Britons and drop-kicking druids. He plans to destroy Boudicca and vanquish the Celts in the name of Nero, winning himself the award for "Best Governor of Britain".

"For the glory of Rome!"

Paulinus is commanded to put an end to Boudicca's rebellion.

Make the Punishment Fit the Crime

The Roman Army had "discipline". They did what they were told, every time. And if they didn't do as they were told – no matter how small the offence – they had to be punished.

You have to fight for Rome, which is a real pain in the neck. If you don't it's a real pain in the neck…

Atti is captured as a deserter and faces his punishment.

PLOPICUS

CRIME	PUNISHMENT
Laziness 	Sleep outside the safety of the camp
Falling asleep on duty	Get the worst food – rough barley instead of good corn
Running away in a battle	Death by beating
Putting your unit in danger	Death by stoning
Running away from your unit	Decimation of a unit – I man in every X is executed

BARBARIC BRITONS

THE BATTLING BRITONS

If you weren't a Roman then the Romans called you "barbarian". This was because the Romans didn't understand the language of strange peoples. They said they sounded like sheep – "bah-bah-bah" people ... bah-bah-rians ... barbarians, get it?

So, when the Romans arrived in Britain they met "barbarians". But the Britons weren't "barbarous" they weren't rough, crude, simple people. They were simply "different".

TERRIBLE TIMELINE

BC

BC 70
Druids are becoming powerful leaders of the Britons.

BC 55
Julius Caesar invades but doesn't stay for long.

AD

10 AD
Britain independent from Rome but some British leaders like to copy Roman way of life.

30 AD
The rich south-east of Britain under one ruler – Cunobelinus – who gives himself the Roman name of "Rex", meaning "King".

41 AD
Cunobelinus dies; his sons Togodumnus and Caratacus take over. They're not so keen on the Romans.

42 AD Verica (king of the Atribates in southern England) is thrown out by his people because he is friendly with Rome. (Caratacus was stirring them up!) Verica flees to Rome and asks for Roman help.

43 AD

The Romans invade and Togodomnus is killed after a battle at the River Medway.

51 AD

After years of resistance Caratacus is betrayed and handed over to the Romans in chains.

60 AD

Queen of the Iceni in East Anglia, Boudicca, leads a rebellion against the Romans and is defeated.

122 AD

Emperor Hadrian's wall is begun, to stop the Picts and Scots invading England.

125 AD

Britons are encouraged to join the Roman Army – and become Roman citizens when they retire.

213 AD

All free Britons become Roman citizens – but Roman citizens pay Roman taxes!

367 AD

As the Roman Empire weakens, the attacks on Hadrian's Wall increase.

401 AD

As the Romans begin to leave, their way of life leaves too. Roman coins are replaced by the ancient custom of bartering.

410 AD

The Emperor Honorius tells the Britons, "Defend yourselves," as the Irish, the Picts, the Scots and the Saxons (from north Germany) begin to raid Britain.

420 AD

Saxons begin to settle in eastern Britain.

443 AD

Plagues in the towns help drive people back to the old British ways of country living.

446 AD

The British appeal to Rome for help against the Saxons. No help arrives. The days of Roman Britain are over. The Saxons have the rich south-east. The Britons have to make do with the poor, wild north and west.

ORLA

(played by Emilia Jones)

Orla is a fearless and feisty Celt. Inspired by her idol, Boudicca, she's desperate to prove herself as a warrior to her overprotective father. When she captures a young Roman soldier, she hopes to finally earn her right to have a sword. But things go wrong when a rival tribe kidnaps her gran and she must enlist the help of a Roman. Orla learns that sometimes family and friends are more important than bashing people over the head.

"Look at me! I'm a warrior!"

HOLDING OUT FOR A HAIRDO!

BOUDICCACA

The Romans thought the Britons were all badly dressed, unwashed barbarians. And the stylish Italians weren't wrong. The Celts did have some freaky fashion tips.

The Celtic men were proud of their hair. They bleached it by washing it in lime. The roots of the hair would be dark and the rest a bleached blond. The lime also made the hair stand on end. They went into battle with their hair in a crest of spikes. One writer said the spikes were so stiff and strong that you could have stuck an apple on the end of each point! And they didn't wear helmets that could save their life in a battle – it would have spoiled their hairstyle!

Brave British women must have looked as fearsome as their blue warrior men. They painted their fingernails, reddened their cheeks with a herb called ruan and darkened their eyebrows with the juice of berries.

HAIR TODAY,
GONE TOMORROW!

HEADS YOU WIN, HEADS YOU LOSE

Just like the heads in Orla's prison hut, heads were popular with the Celtic race to which the Britons belonged. Here's a heads-up on some horrible brainless facts…

• In 500 BC, the British tribes people believed that the head had magical powers. They thought that severed heads could utter prophecies and warnings, especially if they were in groups of three.

• Rotting human heads were stuck on poles at the entrance to a hill fort.

• Heads could be thrown into a lake or river as a gift to the gods.

• After a battle the Celts rode from the battlefield with the heads of enemies dangling from the necks of their horses.

• The heads might then be nailed to the walls of their houses.

• Sometimes they were preserved in cedar oil and taken out years later to show off to visitors. A Roman visitor said that the Britons would not part with their lucky heads for their weight in gold.

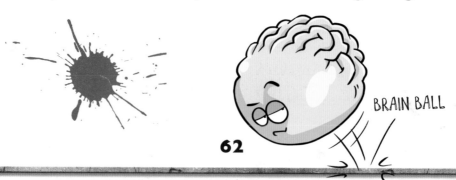

BRAIN BALL

ARGHUS
(played by Nick Frost)

Arghus is Orla's father and the village chief. Unlike his daughter and his mother-in-law, Arghus doesn't think the Romans are all bad. In fact, he's quite partial to a pillar. Arghus struggles to protect his daughter, who wants to run off and fight the Romans with Boudicca. But after the bloodbath at the Battle of Watling Street, he eventually realises that his little Celtic warrior can take care of herself.

"They grow up so fast!"

Arghus is always trying to stop Orla and Brenda from getting into trouble.

BRENDA

(played by Joanna Bacon)

Brenda is Orla's gran and Arghus' mother-in-law. She's feisty and fighty, just like her granddaughter. Brenda has a horrible habit of pilfering other people's possessions, and when her awful actions and outrageous attitude get her into trouble with a rival tribe, she finds herself in a spot of bother. A Roman-hater at heart, her attitude changes when Atti helps to rescue her (but that doesn't stop her from wanting to sacrifice him in the bog).

"Fight, fight, fight!"

THE CUT-THROAT CELTS

The Britons were part of the Celtic people. The Celts used to fight fiercely for their tribal chiefs. But the tribes often fought against each other when they should have been fighting together. They needed one strong leader to bring them all together.

Then Big Boud came along. Boudicca was married to King Prasutagus of the Iceni tribe. Under Roman Law Boudicca, as a woman, had no right to inherit her husband's property. After Prasutagus died, the Romans came and took the lot.

This made Boudicca angry. And the Romans wouldn't like her when she was angry… Boudicca united Briton tribes and led them in an uprising against the rotten Roman army.

BOUDICCA
(played by Kate Nash)

Big hair and even bigger attitude, Boudicca is one Celt that you don't want to cross. After the death of her husband, Prasutagus, Boudicca becomes queen of the Iceni tribe of Britons. But when the Romans pull a fast one, the warrior queen turns against her Roman masters and unleashes her wrecking ball on Colchester, St Albans and London. With a song in her heart and a sword in her hand, she lights up the battlefield – literally.

"RAHHHH!"

Big Hair, Big Attitude

Boudicca always looked pretty fearsome with her huge mop of bright red hair, her rough voice and her king-sized body. A Roman writer, Cassius Dio, said…

"She was very tall. Her eyes seemed to stab you. Her voice was harsh and loud. Her thick, reddish-brown hair hung down below her waist. She always wore a great golden torc [band] around her neck and a flowing tartan cloak fastened with a brooch."

BOUDICCA'S ARMY

To inspire the Celt tribes, Big Boud rode round the Brit tribes in her war chariot and gave them her famous speech…

"We British are used to women commanders in war. I am the daughter of mighty men. But I am not fighting for my royal power now… I am fighting as an ordinary person who has lost her freedom. I am fighting for my bruised body. The gods will grant us the revenge we deserve. Think of how many of us are fighting, and why. Then you will win this battle or die. That is what I, a woman, plan to do. Let the men live as slaves if they want. I won't!"

BLOODY BATTLES

The revolting Britons captured the Roman towns of Camulodunum (now called Colchester in Essex) and burned it to the ground.

Big Boud marched on to Londinium (London) and Verulamium (St Albans) where her army did a lot of murdering and pillaging. In all they killed about 70,000 people. However, one Roman – Paulinus – didn't run away.

At the Battle of Watling Street, Paulinus and the Roman army took a stand against Boudicca's army. Paulinus had just 10,000 soldiers to fight 100,000 Brits. The 10,000 Romans were well organised. The 100,000 Britons charged around the way they always did. The result was a great victory for the Romans.

Atti's bottleneck plan means disaster for the Celts.

BOUDICCA,
THAT WAS YOUR LIFE!

After Big Boud's defeat at Watling Street, the Roman historian, Tacitus, said she took poison and died. Whereas the Roman historian, Dio, said she died of a disease. Believe whichever one you like … or neither. Perhaps she just died of a broken heart.

Tacitus said 80,000 Brit warriors had been killed in Boudicca's final battle. That means each of the 10,000 Roman soldiers killed (on average) eight Britons! He claimed that only 400 Romans died so it took 250 Britons to kill just one Roman! No wonder the British lost!

Of course, the fact is that Tacitus was telling fibs. He wanted to tell the Roman world what a great army the Romans had and how brave their leaders were … after all, his father-in-law was one of those fighting in that battle!

So, DON'T believe everything you read in your history books. If the Brits had been able to write then, they would have given a very different account of the battle.

BOUDICCACA

Big Boud is defeated at the Battle of Watling Street.

THAT STAINY BIT

This is Britain, they don't have sun and it rains all the time ... the Brits do have some good bogs, though!

The Celtic scenes were filmed at Butser Ancient Farm, Waterlooville (Orla's village), Celtic Harmony Camp, Hertford (Boudicca's village) and Burnham Beeches (Enemy camp).

AND THE REST IS HISTORY...

The Romans lived in savage times. They had better roads and laws and weapons and leaders than their enemies – the people they called the "barbarians". And the ancient Romans are rightly remembered for their cleverness – so clever we can look back at their history and still be amazed. Look at their ruins and wonder how they built such great things as Hadrian's Wall or the Colosseum 2,000 years ago. Just don't be blinded by their cleverness. The real secret of their success was that they could be more savage than their cruellest enemies ... totally rotten Romans!

Atti and Orla learn that Celts aren't all wild
and Romans aren't all mean.

Gruesome Gallery

LIGHTS, CAMERA, ACTION – WAIT, WHAT'S A CAMERA?

No Romans, Britons or rats were harmed in the making of this movie.

⌈HORRIBLE HISTORIES⌉

®

AUTHOR AND ILLUSTRATOR

Terry Deary was born at a very early age, so long ago he can't remember. But his mother, who was there at the time, says he was born in Sunderland, north-east England, in 1946 – so it's not true that he writes all Horrible Histories from memory. At school he was a horrible child only interested in playing football and giving teachers a hard time. His history lessons were so boring and so badly taught, that he learned to loathe the subject. Horrible Histories is his revenge.

Martin Brown was born in Melbourne, on the proper side of the world. Ever since he can remember he's been drawing. His dad used to bring back huge sheets of paper from work and Martin would fill them with doodles and little figures. Then, quite suddenly, with food and water, he grew up, moved to the UK and found work doing what he's always wanted to do: drawing doodles and little figures.